STARTING A BUSINESS FAST GUIDE 4 BEGINNERS 2024:The Ultimate Guide for Beginners

ROBERT Y SMITH

1

About the Author

Robert Y Smith is an experienced entrepreneur, business coach, and author with over 20 years of experience in the business world. He has successfully started and grown multiple businesses in a variety of industries, including technology, retail, and consulting. Robert is passionate about helping aspiring entrepreneurs achieve their dreams of starting and growing successful businesses.

Robert's journey as an entrepreneur began at a young age when he started his first business selling handmade jewelry. Since then, he has gone on to start and grow several successful businesses, including a technology consulting firm and a retail store. Along the way, he has learned valuable lessons about what it takes to succeed in business and is eager to share his knowledge and experience with others.

In addition to his work as an entrepreneur, Robert is also a dedicated business coach and mentor. He has helped countless aspiring entrepreneurs turn their ideas into successful businesses and is committed to helping others achieve their goals.

Robert is also an accomplished author, having written several books on entrepreneurship and business success. His latest book, "Starting a Business Fast Guide for Beginners 2024," is a comprehensive guide to starting and growing a successful business. In this book, Robert shares his insights and strategies for success, drawing on his own experiences as an entrepreneur and business coach.

Robert is passionate about helping others achieve their dreams of starting and growing successful businesses. He believes that with the right mindset, strategies, and support, anyone can achieve success as an entrepreneur. Whether you're just starting or looking to take your business to the next level, Robert's books and coaching services can help you achieve your

gIntroduction

All through these pages, you'll find the major standards of beginning and growing a business, from refining your underlying plan to sending off your endeavor and then some. Whether you're an old pro hoping to change into business or a novice anxious to investigate the universe of business possession, this guide is for you.

Beginning a business isn't just about bringing in cash; it's tied in with chasing after your interests, making an incentive for other people, and leaving an enduring effect on the world. As you embark on this intriguing excursion, recall that each step you take, regardless of how little, brings you close together. beginning a business can appear to be an overwhelming errand.
Nonetheless, with the right direction and assets available to you, you can explore the intricacies of the business venture and develop an effective business starting from the earliest stage. This guide is intended to be your guide, offering useful bits of knowledge, noteworthy stages, and priceless tips to speed up your way to pioneering achievement.

CHAPTER 1:

Transforming the Idea to Actual Reality

Beginning a business is an intriguing excursion that starts with a dream. The flash touches off the fire of business ventures. In any case, transforming that vision into reality requires cautious preparation, commitment, and difficult work. In this part, we'll investigate the means you want to take to change your business thought into a flourishing endeavor.

1. **Characterize Your Vision**: Your vision is the underpinning of your business. It's the 10,000-foot view of what you need to accomplish. Carve out the opportunity to characterize your vision. Ask yourself inquiries like: What issue am I addressing? Who is my ideal interest group? What makes my business exceptional? Your vision will direct you through the high points and low points of business ventures.

2. **Direct Statistical surveying:** Before you plunge into beginning your business, understanding your market is fundamental. Direct careful statistical surveying to recognize your main interest group, contenders, and industry patterns. This will assist you with settling on informed choices and position your business for progress.

3. **Make a Field-tested strategy:** A field-tested strategy is a guide that frames your business objectives, methodologies, and monetary projections. A significant report will direct you through the beginning phases of your business. Your field-tested strategy ought to incorporate a leader outline, organization portrayal, market investigation, showcasing and deals methodologies, and monetary projections.

4. **Pick a Business Design:** The construction of your business will influence your legitimate and burdened commitments. Normal business structures incorporate sole ownership, organization, enterprise, and restricted risk

organization (LLC). Consider talking with a lawful or monetary guide to decide the best design for your business.

5. **Register Your Business:** Whenever you've picked a business structure, you'll have to enroll your business with the proper government specialists. This normally includes getting a permit to operate, enlisting your business name, and getting any vital grants or certificates.

6. **Set Up Your Funds:** Legitimate monetary administration is essential for the progress of your business. Set up a different business financial balance, track your costs, and make a spending plan. Consider recruiting a bookkeeper or utilizing bookkeeping programming to assist you with dealing with your funds.

7. **Construct Your Image:** Your image is how your clients see your business. Critical to make major areas of strength for a character mirror your vision and values. This incorporates planning a logo, making a site, and fostering a showcasing system.

8. **Send off Your Business:** Whenever you've finished the vital arrangements, now is the right time to send off your business. This might include facilitating a send-off occasion, advancing your business via online entertainment, or contacting likely clients.

9. **Screen and Adjust:** Beginning a business is a powerful cycle that requires consistent observing and transformation. Watch out for your funds, keep tabs on your development, and be ready to make changes on a case-by-case basis.

10. **Look for Help:** Beginning a business can be testing, however you don't need to do it single-handedly. Look for help from tutors, counselors, and different business visionaries. Join organizing gatherings, go to studios, and exploit assets accessible to you.

Keep in mind that beginning a business is an excursion, not an objective. Keep fixed on your vision, be ready to adjust, and learn constantly. With commitment and determination, you can transform your vision into the real world and fabricate an effective business.

Chapter 2:

Financial Awareness for Narrative

In this section, we'll dig into the monetary parts of beginning and maintaining a true-to-life business. From planning to overseeing income, we'll investigate the key monetary contemplations that each genuine business person ought to know about.

1. **Planning:** Planning is the groundwork of monetary administration for any business. It includes assessing your pay and costs and assigning assets as needed. Begin by making a financial plan that frames your normal income and costs for the year. Make certain to incorporate both fixed costs (e.g., lease, utilities) and variable expenses (e.g., advertising, supplies). Audit your spending plan routinely and make changes depending on the situation.

2. **Overseeing Income**: Income is the backbone of your business. It's the development of cash all

through your business, and it's fundamental to really oversee it. Monitor your income by checking your records receivable (cash owed to you) and records payable (cash you owe). Consider carrying out an income using the board framework to assist you with keeping steady over your funds.

3. **Estimating Your Items or Administrations:** Valuing is a basic part of your business methodology. Critical to set costs to cover your expenses and create a benefit. Consider factors, for example, your objective market, rivalry, and incentive while deciding your valuing system. Make certain to consistently survey and change your costs depending on the situation.

4. **Figuring out Net revenues:** Net revenues are critical to your business's monetary well-being. They address the level of income that is left in the wake of deducting costs. Understanding your overall revenues can assist you with settling on informed conclusions about evaluating, cost administration, and development systems.

5. **Overseeing Obligation:** Obligation can be a helpful device for funding your business, yet it's essential to mindfully oversee it. Be vital about assuming obligation and consider factors, for example, loan fees, reimbursement terms, and the effect on your income. Foster an arrangement for taking care of obligation and try not to assume more obligation than you can serenely make due.

6. **Charge Arranging:** Duties are an unavoidable piece of maintaining a business, yet there are ways of limiting your expense risk. Consider working with an expense proficient to foster a duty procedure that exploits accessible derivations and credits. Make certain to keep precise records and document your assessments on the chance to stay away from punishments.

7. **Building a Just-in-case account:** Surprising costs can emerge whenever, so it's critical to have a secret stash to cover them. This means saving three to a half years of costs in a different

investment account. This will give a monetary pad and genuine serenity in the event of crises.

8. **Putting resources into Development:** As your business develops, you might have to put resources into extra assets, like gear, innovation, or workforce. Be key about these speculations and consider factors like profit from venture (return for capital invested) and long haul development potential.

9. **Observing Monetary Execution:** Routinely checking your monetary exhibition is fundamental for pursuing informed choices and distinguishing regions for development. Utilize fiscal summaries, for example, pay explanations, accounting reports, and income proclamations to keep tabs on your development and distinguish patterns.

10. **Looking for Proficient Counsel:** Monetary administration can be complicated, so go ahead and proficient exhortation when required. Think about working with a monetary consultant,

bookkeeper, or clerk to assist you with exploring the monetary parts of your business.

By getting it and dealing with the monetary parts of your verifiable business, you'll be better prepared to settle on informed choices and construct an effective undertaking. Keep in mind, that monetary clever is an expertise that can be created over the long haul, so make sure to clarify some things, look for exhortation, and learn.

Chapter 3:

Specific Factors to be Considered: Group Formation and Recruitment

In this part, we'll investigate the significance of employing and group working in building a fruitful verifiable business. From finding the right ability to encouraging a positive work culture, we'll examine the vital contemplations for making areas of strength for a firm group.

1. **Characterize Your Group Needs:** Before you begin recruiting, it's vital to characterize your group needs. Consider factors, for example, the size of your business, the abilities and mastery required, and your spending plan. Make a rundown of the jobs and obligations you want to fill and focus on them given your business objectives.

2. **Make an Expected set of responsibilities:** An elegantly composed set of working responsibilities is fundamental for drawing in the right competitors. Be clear about the capabilities,

abilities, and experience you're searching for, as well as the obligations and assumptions for the job. Consider including data about your organization's culture and values to draw in up-and-comers who line up with your vision.

3. **Source Competitors:** There are numerous ways of obtaining up-and-comers, including position sheets, web-based entertainment, organizing occasions, and references. Think about utilizing a blend of these strategies to arrive at a different pool of up-and-comers. Make certain to screen applicants cautiously and direct meetings to evaluate their abilities, experience, and fit with your group.

4. **Direct Meetings:** Meetings are a potential chance to get to know up-and-comers and evaluate their appropriateness for the job. Set up a rundown of inquiries that will assist you with assessing their abilities, experience, and fit with your group. Think about leading different rounds of meetings to get a thorough perspective on every up-and-comer.

5. **Make a Proposition:** Whenever you've recognized the right competitor, now is the ideal time to make a deal. Be clear about the terms of business, including pay, advantages, and begin date. Consider haggling with the contender to guarantee a commonly gainful understanding.

6. **Locally available New Workers:** Onboarding is a significant interaction for incorporating new representatives into your group. Furnish them with the data, assets, and backing they should find actual success in their job. Consider doling out a guide or pal to assist them with exploring their initial not many weeks.

7. **Encourage a Positive Work Culture:** A positive work culture is fundamental for drawing in and holding top ability. Establish a workplace that is comprehensive, steady, and deferential. Support open correspondence, cooperation, and criticism. Consider executing advantages and advantages that advance the balance between fun

and serious activities and representative prosperity.

8. **Foster Your Group:** Putting resources into the improvement of your group is fundamental for building major areas of strength for a durable group. Give chances to prepare, proficient turn of events, and ability building. Urge representatives to define objectives and furnish them with the help they need to accomplish them.

9. **Oversee Execution**: Routinely audit and deal with your colleagues. Give criticism, put forth objectives, and perceive accomplishments. Address any exhibition issues speedily and helpfully. Consider carrying out an exhibition of the board framework to follow the progress and recognize regions for development.

10. **Hold Your Group:** Holding top ability is fundamental for the drawn-out progress of your business. Be proactive about tending to representative worries and giving open doors to

development and headway. Consider executing maintenance procedures like cutthroat compensations, advantages, and advantages.

By zeroing in on employing and group building, you'll be better prepared to fabricate serious areas of strength for a durable group that can assist you with accomplishing your business objectives. Keep in mind, that your group is your most significant resource, so put resources into their turn of events and prosper.

Chapter 4:

The Craft of Authority in a Primary Company

Leadership in a small business is an art, not a science. It's about understanding and inspiring others, fostering a positive and productive work environment, and navigating challenges with a clear vision and steady hand. This chapter will equip you with the essential tools and knowledge to master this art form and unlock the full potential of your venture.

The Pillars of Small Business Leadership:

Four key pillars underpin successful leadership in small businesses:

1. **Vision and Inspiration**: A clear and compelling vision serves as a roadmap for your business and a motivator for your team. Articulate your vision concisely, communicate it passionately, and weave it

into your daily operations. Remember, inspiration is contagious – spark it within yourself and it will ignite others.

2. **Empowerment and Delegation:** Don't try to be a superhero! Trust your team members by delegating tasks that match their skills and interests. Provide clear expectations, support, and constructive feedback to help them thrive. This empowers them to take ownership and contribute their unique talents, ultimately leading to a stronger, more collaborative team.

3. **Communication and Transparency:** Open and honest communication is the lifeblood of any successful team. Regularly share information about goals, challenges, and successes. Encourage questions and feedback, creating a safe space for open dialogue. Remember, transparency builds trust and fosters a sense of shared purpose.

Recognition and Appreciation: Acknowledge and celebrate the achievements of your team, big and small. A simple "thank you" or a public shout-out can go a long way in boosting morale and motivating continued excellence. Recognition shows your team members that their contributions are valued, fostering loyalty and engagement.

Leading in Today's Dynamic Landscape:

The year 2024 brings unique challenges and opportunities for small business leaders. Here are some key considerations:

4. **Embrace Remote Work:** With advancements in technology, remote work models are becoming increasingly prevalent. If applicable, consider offering flexible work arrangements to attract and retain top talent. Ensure clear communication, effective collaboration tools, and a culture of trust to make remote work successful.

Prioritize Diversity and Inclusion: Building a diverse and inclusive team fosters creativity, innovation, and stronger connections with your customer base. Actively seek diverse perspectives, celebrate differences, and create a work environment where everyone feels valued and respected.

Promote Agility and Adaptability: The business landscape is constantly evolving. Be prepared to adapt your strategies, embrace new technologies, and learn from challenges. Encourage a culture of continuous learning and experimentation within your team.

5. **Bonus Tip Lead by Example:** Your actions speak louder than words. Be the embodiment of the values you expect from your team. Demonstrate integrity, work ethic, and a positive attitude. Your leadership style will set the tone for your entire organization.

Remember: Small business leadership is a journey, not a destination. Embrace continuous learning, be open to feedback, and celebrate your successes along the way. By mastering the art of leadership, you'll create a thriving environment where your team can flourish and your business can reach its full potential.

Chapter 5:

Showcasing Your Business

In this part, we'll investigate the significance of showcasing in developing your private company. From building brand attention to drawing in new clients, we'll talk about the vital systems and strategies that can assist you with actually promoting your business.

1. **Define Your Objective Audience:** The most vital phase in showcasing your business is to characterize your ideal interest group. Who are your optimal clients? What are their requirements, inclinations, and trouble spots? Understanding your interest group will assist you with fitting your promoting endeavors to successfully contact them.

2. **Create a Promoting Plan:** A showcasing plan is a guide that frames your showcasing objectives, procedures, and strategies. It ought to incorporate a point-by-point examination of your

interest groups, a serious investigation, a spending plan, and a course of events. Your showcasing plan will direct your promoting endeavors and assist you with estimating your prosperity.

3. **Build Your Brand:** Your image is the way your clients see your business. Critical to make serious areas of strength for a personality that mirrors your vision and values. This incorporates planning a logo, making a site, and fostering a showcasing procedure.

4. **Develop a Substance Strategy:** Content showcasing is an incredible asset for drawing in and connecting with your interest group. Foster a substance technique that incorporates making significant, pertinent, and steady happy that resounds with your crowd. This can incorporate blog entries, virtual entertainment posts, recordings, and that's just the beginning.

5. **Leverage Social Media:** Virtual entertainment is an important showcasing

instrument for independent ventures. It permits you to associate with your crowd, fabricate connections, and advance your items or administrations. Pick the online entertainment stages that are generally pertinent to your main interest group and make a substance schedule to guarantee predictable posting.

6. **Optimize Your Website:** Your site is much of the time the initial feeling clients have of your business. Ensure it's easy to use, portable responsive, and streamlined for web search tools. Use catchphrases applicable to your business to further develop your web crawler positioning and draw in more natural rush hour gridlock.

7. **Use Email Marketing:** Email promoting is a practical method for contacting your crowd and fabricating associations with them. Make an email rundown of intrigued clients and send them customary updates, advancements, and important substance.

8. **Leverage Influencers:** Powerhouse promoting is a strong method for contacting new crowds and fabricating believability for your image. Recognize powerhouses in your industry who have an enormous following and draw in with them to advance your items or administrations.

9. **Monitor and Measure Your Results:** It means quite a bit to screen and quantify the consequences of your promoting endeavors. Use examination instruments to follow your site traffic, online entertainment commitment, and email open rates, and the sky is the limit from there. Utilize this information to go with informed choices and change your advertising technique depending on the situation.

10. **Stay In the Know regarding Trends:** The advertising scene is continually developing, so keeping awake to-date with the most recent patterns and best practices is significant. Follow industry web journals, go to online classes, and

organize with different advertisers to remain educated and on the ball.

By zeroing in on these critical systems and strategies, you'll be better prepared to advertise your private venture and draw in new clients. Keep in mind, that promoting is a continuous cycle, so be patient and persevering in your endeavors.

Chapter 6:

Offering Your Business to Progress

In this part, we'll investigate the craft of offering your business to progress. From understanding your client's requirements to finalizing the negotiation, we'll examine the vital techniques and strategies that can assist you with actually selling your items or administrations.

1. **Understand Your Clients' Needs:** The most vital phase in offering your business to progress is to grasp your client's necessities. What issues would they say they are attempting to tackle? What are their trouble spots? By understanding your clients' necessities, you can fit your items or administrations to successfully meet them.

2. **Create a Remarkable Worth Proposition:** An exceptional incentive separates your business from the opposition. It's the motivation behind why clients ought to pick your items or administrations over others. Foster an

unmistakable and convincing incentive that resounds with your main interest group.

3. **Identify Your Optimal Customers:** Not all clients are made equivalent. Recognize your optimal clients - the people who are probably going to profit from your items or administrations and who will pay for them. Center your advertising endeavors around coming to and drawing in these clients.

4. **Build Relationships:** Building associations with your clients is fundamental for offering your business to progress. Draw in with them via web-based entertainment, answer their inquiries and criticism, and give fantastic client support. Building trust and affinity with your clients will make them bound to purchase from you.

5. **Leverage Tributes and Reviews:** Tributes and audits are useful assets for offering your business to progress. They give social confirmation that your items or administrations are important and successful. Urge fulfilled

clients to leave surveys and tributes, and use them in your showcasing materials.

6. **Offer Incentives:** Impetuses can be a strong inspiration for clients to purchase from you. Offer limits, advancements, or gifts to urge clients to make a buy. Be vital about when and how you offer motivating forces to augment their effect.

7. **Provide Brilliant Client Service:** Great client care is fundamental for offering your business to progress. Answer client requests and concerns expeditiously and expertly. Exceed everyone's expectations to surpass your client's assumptions and make a positive encounter.

8. **Use Upselling and Cross-Selling:** Upselling and strategically pitching are powerful systems for expanding the worth of every client exchange. Offer reciprocal items or administrations that upgrade the client's insight or take care of unexpected issues. Be key about how you present these proposals to clients.

9. **Close the Deal:** Settling the negotiation is the last move toward offering your business to progress. Be certain, powerful, and clear in your correspondence. Address any protests or concerns the client might have and give consolation. Make it simple for the client to finish the buy.

10. **Follow-Up:** Circling back to clients after the deal is fundamental for building long-haul connections and rehashing business. Say thanks to them for their buy, request input, and proposition of extra help or assets. Show that you esteem their business and are focused on their fulfillment.

By zeroing in on these critical systems and strategies, you'll be better prepared to offer your business to progress. Keep in mind, that selling is a cycle, not a one-time occasion. Constantly refine and further develop your business systems to boost your prosperity.

Chapter 7:

Exploring the Business Visionary Way

In this part, we'll investigate the excursion of a business venture and the significance of driving from the front. From facing challenges to embracing disappointment, we'll talk about the vital characteristics and methodologies that can assist you with exploring the business visionary way effectively.

1. **Embrace Risk:** A business venture is intrinsically hazardous, but at the same time it's brimming with open doors. Embrace risk and go ahead with carefully thought-out plans of action to accomplish your objectives. Be ready to step outside your usual range of familiarity and attempt new things.

2. **Be Resilient:** A business venture is an excursion loaded up with high points and low points. Be tough and return from difficulties and

disappointments. Gain from your missteps and use them as any open doors for development.

3. **Stay Focused:** Business venture requires concentration and discipline. Remain fixed on your objectives and needs, and try not to get occupied by gleaming articles. Foster a reasonable arrangement and stick to it.

4. **Be Adaptable:** The business scene is continually changing, and as a business person, you should be versatile. Be available to novel thoughts and approaches, and turn when vital.

5. **Lead by Example:** As a business visionary, you set the vibe for your group. Show others how it's done by exhibiting the qualities and ways of behaving you anticipate from your group. Tell the truth, be moral, and be responsible in your activities.

6. **Be Passionate:** Energy is a critical driver of outcomes in business ventures. Be enthusiastic

about your vision and your business, and let that energy fuel your activities and choices.

7. **Build a Solid Team:** Encircle yourself with a solid group of gifted people who share your vision and values. Delegate errands and obligations, and enable your group to take responsibility for work.

8. **Seek Feedback:** Criticism is fundamental for development and improvement. Look for criticism from clients, tutors, and consultants, and use it to refine and work on your business.

9. **Stay Curious:** A business venture is an excursion of ceaseless learning and development. Remain inquisitive and receptive, and gain from others and from your encounters.

10. **Celebrate Successes:** Business can be testing, so praising your victories en route is significant. Carve out opportunities to recognize and commend your accomplishments, and use them as inspiration to continue to push forward.

By zeroing in on these critical characteristics and methodologies, you'll be better prepared to effectively explore the business person way. Keep in mind, a business venture is an excursion, not an objective. Remain on track, remain tough, and continue to push forward, and you'll accomplish your objectives.

Chapter 8:

Expanding Your Business: Optimal Timing, Strategic Planning, and Effective Implementation

In this section, we'll dig into the complexities of scaling your business, zeroing in on the basic parts of timing, readiness, and execution. Scaling a business isn't just about development; it's tied in with doing so in a key and manageable way. How about we investigate how to successfully explore this excursion?

1. **Optimal Timing:** Timing is significant in scaling your business. It's essential to scale with flawless timing when your business is prepared for development. This implies having a strong groundwork, a demonstrated item or administration, and an unmistakable comprehension of your market and clients.

2. **Strategic Planning:** Arrangement is fundamental for effective scaling. This includes

leading exhaustive statistical surveying, fostering a reasonable development methodology, and building areas of strength for a. It additionally implies having the right situation and cycles set up to help development, like versatile innovation arrangements and proficient tasks.

3. **Effective Implementation:** Implementation is where everything becomes real concerning scaling your business. It's essential to execute your development methodology really and effectively. This implies keeping fixed on your objectives, being versatile, and going with information-driven choices. It likewise implies being ready to turn when vital and being willing to go ahead with well-balanced plans of action.

4. **Focus on Client Experience:** As you scale your business, it's essential to keep an emphasis on client experience. Giving an uncommon client experience is fundamental for holding clients and drawing in new ones. This implies conveying great items or administrations, giving

superb client assistance, and paying attention to client input.

5. **Optimize Your Operations:** Smoothing out your activities can assist you with scaling your business all the more proficiently. Recognize regions where you can further develop effectiveness, lessen expenses, and increment efficiency. This might incorporate mechanizing redundant assignments and re-appropriating non-center capabilities, and that's just the beginning.

6. **Monitor and Measure Your Progress:** Consistently screen and measure your advancement towards your objectives. Utilize key execution pointers (KPIs) to follow your exhibition and distinguish regions for development. Utilize this information to settle on informed choices and change your procedure depending on the situation.

7. **Be Patient and Persistent:** Scaling your business takes time and exertion. Be patient and

industrious, and be encouraged by difficulties or difficulties. Remain fixed on your objectives and continue to push forward, and you'll make progress.

By zeroing in on these critical parts of timing, readiness, and execution, you'll be better prepared to scale your business really and accomplish your objectives. Keep in mind, that scaling your business is an excursion, not an objective. Remain on track, remain tough, and continue to push forward, and you'll accomplish your objectives.

Chapter 9:

Encouraging Advancement and Flexibility

In this section, we'll investigate the significance of encouraging advancement and flexibility in your business. From embracing change to empowering inventiveness, we'll talk about the critical systems and strategies that can assist you with remaining on the ball and driving development.

1. **Embrace Change:** Change is unavoidable in business, and it's essential to embrace it as opposed to oppose it. Be available to novel thoughts, advances, and approaches. Urge your group to think imaginatively and attempt new things.

2. **Encourage Creativity:** Inventiveness is fundamental for development. Urge your group to break new ground and concoct novel thoughts. Establish a workplace that cultivates

innovativeness, for example, by giving chances to conceptualize and coordinate efforts.

3. **Stay Informed:** Remain informed about industry patterns, mechanical headways, and changes on the lookout. Go to gatherings, read industry distributions, and organize with different experts. Utilize this information to distinguish potential open doors for development and development.

4. **Invest in Exploration and Development:** Putting resources into innovative work (Research and Development) is fundamental for encouraging advancement. Designate assets for Research and development endeavors that line up with your business objectives and ideal interest group. This might incorporate growing new items or administrations, working on existing ones, or investigating new business sectors.

5. **Be Adaptable:** The business scene is continually changing, and as an entrepreneur,

you should be versatile. Be available to novel thoughts and approaches, and turn when essential. This might include changing your plan of action, entering new business sectors, or taking on new innovations.

6. **Encourage Chance-Taking:** Going ahead with potentially dangerous courses of action is fundamental for development. Urge your group to face challenges and attempt new things. Give them the help and assets they need to explore and gain from their encounters.

7. **Reward Innovation:** Compensating development can assist with cultivating a culture of innovativeness and risk-taking. Perceive and celebrate representatives who concoct novel thoughts or make critical commitments to the business. Consider carrying out a prizes program or offering motivators for development.

8. **Create a Culture of Learning:** A culture of learning is fundamental for encouraging development and versatility. Urge your group to

constantly learn and develop, both actually and expertly. Give amazing chances to prepare, proficient turn of events, and ability building.

9. **Lead by Example:** As an entrepreneur, you set the vibe for your group. Show others how it's done by exhibiting an eagerness to learn, adjust, and enhance. Be available to groundbreaking thoughts and approaches, and face challenges.

10. **Stay Client-Centric:** Advancement ought to be driven by the necessities and inclinations of your clients. Remain client-driven by routinely requesting criticism, leading statistical surveying, and remaining informed about your ideal interest group. Utilize this data to direct your advancement endeavors and guarantee that they line up with your client's requirements.

By zeroing in on these critical methodologies and strategies, you'll be better prepared to cultivate development and versatility in your business. Keep in mind, that development is an excursion, not an objective. Remain on track, remain versatile, and continue to push forward, and you'll accomplish your objectives.

Conclusion:

Starting a Business Fast Guide for Beginners 2024

Starting a business is a thrilling excursion, but at the same time it's a difficult one. It requires commitment, difficult work, and an eagerness to learn and adjust. Yet, with the right mentality and the right procedures, you can transform your vision into the real world and fabricate an effective business that has a constructive outcome on the world.

Keep in mind, that business is an excursion, not an objective. It's essential to remain fixed on your objectives, remain strong notwithstanding difficulties, and continue to push forward. What's more, above all, make it a point to request help. Encircle yourself with a solid encouraging group of people of coaches, counsels, and individual business visionaries who can give direction and back route.

Much obliged to you for going along with us on this excursion. We hope everything works out for you of karma in your pioneering attempts. Keep in mind, that the sky's the cutoff, and with the right mentality and the right procedures, you can accomplish anything you put your energy into. Best of luck!